People of Early Scotland

People of Early Scotland

from contemporary images

Anna Ritchie
Ian G Scott and Tom E Gray

The Pinkfoot Press
Brechin
2006

First published 2006 in Scotland by

The Pinkfoot Press

1 Pearse Street, Brechin, Angus DD9 6JR

ISBN 1 874012 50 4

*In memory of Graham
and happy years of shared archaeology*

Cover design by David Henry

Designed at The Pinkfoot Press
Printed by The Cromwell Press, Trowbridge

Contents

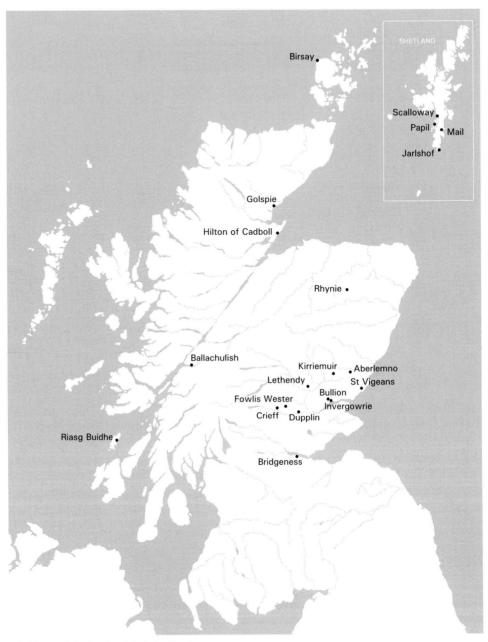

1 *Places of the People of Early Scotland*

Introduction

Portraiture has been an essential element of Scottish art in recent centuries but it was not always so. Scotland has none of the plump ladies interpreted as Mother Goddesses that appear in earlier contexts in European prehistory, and the rarity of human representation in local indigenous culture before the mid first millennium AD is puzzling to say the least. Rock art was prolific in the west of Scotland in the third and second millennia BC, but its creators favoured circular hollows or cup-marks, often surrounded by grooved rings, rather than the narrative art seen in Scandinavia and Atlantic Europe with human figures, animals and boats. There painting as well as carving was used, though the paint survives only in caves. Scottish caves were certainly used from earliest times onward, for shelter and as portals to the spirit world, but none has yielded any trace of art datable before the late Iron Age. Despite the richness of early Celtic art, pictorial realism played a very small part, and it centred upon the human head, birds and animals, rendered mostly in metal and mostly in the round. Carved stone heads were relatively common in the Iron Age of Ireland and Britain but not, apparently, in Scotland. The catalyst for the development of Scottish figural art was Christianity, to which secular society was thoroughly converted by AD 700. Aside from its spiritual teaching, Christianity brought literacy and a long history of artistic development which in Britain and Ireland was to result in all the splendours of Insular art, expressed through illustrated manuscripts, metalwork and sculpture. Imported ideas blended with indigenous taste in decoration, and a full narrative art emerged with realistic depictions of human figures, birds and animals.

The images presented here span some 1600 years from the earliest, the wooden figure from Ballachulish, around 600 BC to the Invergowrie cross-slab of the 9th century AD. All are indigenous works, except for the Roman carving from Bridgeness, included both for its representation of native 'barbarians' and to remind us of the potential influence of Roman art upon the development of late Iron Age art at least in central Scotland. The great lioness devouring human prey found in the River Almond at Cramond had marked the tomb of a senior officer in the Roman army and survived, like the crumbling walls of the fort, long after the army had left, to the marvel of travellers. Throughout these centuries,

Scottish art is dominated by works carved in stone, simply because organic materials have a far lower survival rate, but there would have been images in wood, painted on stone and vellum, and crafted in textiles, straw and basketry.

Scotland has a wonderfully rich heritage of Pictish stone carving, which inevitably dominates this book. The Picts were the descendants of the indigenous tribes whom the Romans encountered in the first century AD, and the historical kingdom of the Picts stretched from the River Forth to Shetland in the far north and to the Western Isles during the 6th to 9th centuries AD. Their conversion to Christianity was a gradual process over the 6th and 7th centuries, and many of the images used here derive from Christian gravestones. Others had a political function, particularly the statement of royal authority embodied in the Dupplin Cross.

Warriors, hunters, warlords and monks are the stone-carvers' most common subjects, but there are also shamans, musicians and just one female in the pages that follow. The images are arranged in broadly chronological order, and at the end of each text is information about where to find the artefact and references to allow you to follow it up in published literature.

Acknowledgements

There would have been no point to this book without the illustrations, and I am deeply grateful to Ian G Scott and Tom E Gray for their generous collaboration. I am also very grateful to the Royal Commission on the Historical Monuments of Scotland, Historic Scotland and the Trustees of the National Museums of Scotland for allowing me to use photographs and drawings in their superb archives and to the photographers and illustrators responsible for their creation. The Tom and Sybil Gray Collection is housed in the RCAHMS archives. I should like to thank Alison Sheridan for her help, Audrey Henshall for her photograph of the Aberlemno cross-slab, Niall Sharples for the photographs of the Mail and Scalloway figures and Isabel and George Henderson for the many inspirations of their published work. David Henry of The Pinkfoot Press encouraged me to persevere with the idea of this book, and I knew that he would transform it into a thing of beauty.

2 *The Ballachulish face as it survives today*
(© Trustees of the National Museums of Scotland)

3 *Engraving of the
figure as found in 1880*
(Christison 1881, fig 1)

The Ballachulish Mother Goddess

A watery grave preserved this wooden figure for some 2400 years. When it was first discovered in November 1880, it looked much the same as when it was first carved in the early Iron Age, but, as the wood dried out, it shrank and became distorted. Nonetheless the figure has a certain presence, and its white quartz eyes still gaze out serenely. It portrays a woman, and the original emphasis upon her genitals was deliberate, a goddess perhaps of the earth mother kind.

She was found in a peat bog at North Ballachulish in what was then northern Argyll and is now part of Highland, close to the sea at the mouth of Loch Leven. Workmen digging through the peat in order to build the foundation for a wall discovered the figure on the gravel at the base of the peat, and the original account describes how 'the image lay on its face, covered with a sort of wicker work; and several pole-like sticks lying near it …'. The wickerwork was 'too frail' to preserve, but it sounds as if it was either part of the shrine in which she had been kept or a device to ensure that she remained pinned down in the bog for eternity. There are no traces of weathering on the figure, which suggests that it was placed in a pit in the bog and covered over with the dug peat, rather than that the peat had grown slowly on top of it. Was her cult in disgrace or was this the vandalism of an enemy tribe with its own preferred fertility deity?

The drawing was made in 1881 from a photograph taken at the time of discovery. She stands ankle-deep in her plinth, and there is a small hollow in the plinth at the point where her feet would be. The hollow may have held some precious object, but nothing was found and we shall never know what it was. There is a faint suggestion of a sash running from her right shoulder towards her hands, and of course, if she had been painted originally, far more detail would have been visible. From the nineteenth century onwards, she has been described as almost life-sized, but in fact the entire figure, goddess and plinth, measured just 4ft 10in (1.47m) in height. Even allowing for the uncarved feet and ankles, this is a diminutive figure. It is, however, considerably taller than most other wooden figures that have survived from prehistoric Britain and Ireland, few in number though they are.

The writer of the original account, Sir Robert Christison, recorded 'It is very slim in figure but not more so than some young ladies of the present day swathed in the swaddling-clothes now in fashion.' An interesting male view of the fashion of the early 1880s! At that time too the Ballachulish goddess was considered too 'indelicate' to be the figure of a saint, and it was therefore attributed to the Scandinavians, those infamous barbarians of the north.

With more advanced scientific methods of analysis, we now know that the figure was carved from alder (rather than oak as used to be thought) and that the wood dates to around 600 BC. This was a time of considerable change in Scotland, when iron-working was being introduced and fortifications were being adopted in response to troubled social times. Statues of mother goddesses carved in stone are common from Celtic times in Britain and Europe, and clearly their names could vary from tribe to tribe. The name of the Ballachulish goddess is lost to us. The Ballachulish figure is a rare survival not only of a wooden artefact but of a 'human' figure, and it gives us a wonderful glimpse of pre-Christian religion in Scotland.

Present location

Museum of Scotland, Chambers Street, Edinburgh.

References

Christison, R 1881 'On an ancient wooden image, found in November last at Ballachulish Peat Moss', *Proc Soc Antiq Scot*, 15 (1880-1), 158–78.

Coles, B 1990 'Anthropomorphic wooden figurines from Britain and Ireland', *Proc Prehist Soc*, 56 (1990), 315–33.

Romans and barbarians at Bridgeness

On 14 April 1868 a villager at Bridgeness, working on extending his vegetable garden, turned over a stone slab and discovered one of the most elaborately decorated Roman inscriptions ever found in Britain. Bridgeness lies between South Queensferry and Grangemouth on the southern shore of the Firth of Forth, close to the point where the building of the Antonine Wall began in AD 142, and this inscription records the completion of the easternmost section of the

4 *Drawing of the Bridgeness slab after its discovery in 1869* (Cadell 1869, pl 7)

Wall. 'For the Emperor Caesar Titus Aelius Hadrianus Antoninus Pius, Father of his Country, the Second Augustan Legion completed over a distance of 4652 paces', the equivalent of 7km today.

Distance slabs, as such inscriptions are known, were set up at either end of each designated length of the Wall by their legionary builders, but this one was particularly special. The scene carved to the right of the inscription shows the *Suovetaurilia*, the sacrifice of a pig (*sus*), a sheep (*ovis*) and a bull (*taurus*),

5 *Detail of the left-hand panel* (© Trustees of the National Museums of Scotland)

that preceded a great military enterprise, and the importance of the occasion is reflected in the size of the slab, for at 2.79m long it is more than a metre longer than any other distance slab to have survived from the Wall.

The battle scene at the other end is a clever study in Roman victory propaganda. Four vanquished Britons are at the mercy of a Roman officer on a prancing horse. They are all naked (to show how barbaric they are) and there will be no mercy, for one has already been wounded in the back by a spear and another lies on the ground trying to protect himself with his shield. In the foreground, we can see what happens to captives after the battle: one has been beheaded and the other sits resigned to the same fate. Abandoned weapons are scattered about and show that, although they were truly warriors with shields, swords and spears, their prowess was inferior to the organised might of the Romans. Compared to these unfortunate Britons, the Roman cavalryman looks overdressed in his tunic, flowing cloak, breastplate, helmet and shoes, as he reins in his horse to spear yet another victim.

On the back of the slab, there are three cramp holes along the top edge and one on each short side, which show that the stone had been fastened to some sort of masonry pedestal, probably set into the south face of the Wall (which was itself built of turf on stone foundations). The stone was cleaned in 1979, and traces of original red paint were found in the letters of the inscription and in the grooves outlining the peltas or crescentic motifs on either side of the central panel. There are also traces of red on the neck of the beheaded prisoner and at the base of his head. It seems likely that other less durable colours of paint were also used and that the two scenes were quite garishly painted.

The easternmost line of the Antonine Wall is uncertain. It used to be thought to end at Bridgeness, but excavations around the find-spot of the inscription have failed to find any trace of Wall or ditch, and the fort at Carriden about a kilometre to the south-east is now seen as the likely terminal. The slab may well have been taken away and re-used as building material, perhaps for the windmill that is known to have preceded the eighteenth-century Bridgeness Tower.

Present location

The findspot of the slab is marked by a nineteenth-century copy of the inscription set into a wall on the west side of Harbour Road, near the junction with Bridgeness Road, Bridgeness, and the slab itself is in the Museum of Scotland, Chambers Street, Edinburgh.

References

Cadell, H M 1869 'Note of a sculptured Roman slab recently discovered on the Estate of Grange, Linlithgowshire, and presented to the Museum', *Proc Soc Antiq Scot*, 8 (1868-9), 109–13.

Keppie, L 2004 *The Legacy of Rome: Scotland's Roman Remains*. Edinburgh.

6 *The Mail figure* (drawing by Ian G Scott; Crown Copyright: RCAHMS)

The shaman of Mail

Unmistakeably pagan in concept, this carving was found in August 1992 by a grave-digger waiting for a funeral party to arrive at the burial ground at Mail in Shetland. A stone slab had been dug up in the graveyard and was lying ready to be used to level up the new coffin, when the carving was noticed and it was put on one side for the Shetland Archaeologist, Val Turner, to see. It was but one in a long series of finds from the area, but the carving is unique, not just in Shetland but in Pictland as a whole. This lightly incised, apparently informal figure with its animal-head seems best explained as a sketch of a Pictish shaman or pagan priest.

The shaman stands 0.44m (1ft 5in) high, in profile facing to the observer's right, as do most such single figures in Pictish art. He makes a portly figure in his knee-length tunic, so much so that George and Isabel Henderson have memorably described his 'bolstered' appearance as 'a straw man fit for burning'. But the eye is drawn to his head, where, instead of a human head, there is an animal's head. With its long jaw and bared teeth it looks like a wolf, and the prominent forehead may suggest that this is a mask worn by the shaman on special occasions. The beard may be the shaman's own. One bare foot before the other to give the impression of walking, he holds a chubby club-like object in his left hand in the way in which one would hold a staff. With his right hand he carries an axe against his shoulder. The axe has quite a slender haft, and the head is clearly that of an axe-hammer. The hem of his tunic is decorated with a band of simple step pattern, probably woven on a braid loom, and the three lines from hem to waist suggest an extra triangle of fabric let into a straight tunic to give greater fullness.

We know very little about Pictish pagan beliefs, but Adomnán's *Life of Columba* describes the saint's tiring journeys from Iona into Pictland, including encounters with the shamans (or *magi* as Adomnán calls them) at the court of the Pictish high king. This is surely the social context for the Mail figure. Animal masks are in keeping with the many carvings of animals, including wolves, on Pictish stones, and the wolf as a fearless predator might be an appropriate guise for communication with the spirit world.

The sandstone slab on which the shaman was sketched was probably

7 *The Mail stone* (drawing by Ian G Scott; Crown Copyright: RCAHMS)

trimmed for later use as a building stone, for there are traces on it of mortar or plaster. It is a thick slab at 0.34m, and its thickness, like the free-hand appearance of the carving, suggests that this was not designed as a formal stone monument, and the carved surface is very uneven. The burial ground where it was found lies on a small promontory that was formerly linked to an islet on which stand the remains of a broch. There was probably a domestic settlement outside the broch on the landward side, underlying the modern graveyard, which would explain the discoveries of buried walls, hearths and ancient artefacts during grave-digging. Like Jarlshof and Old Scatness, the broch village may have continued in occupation into Pictish and Norse times, long after the broch itself went out of use. Other finds from the Mail graveyard include Pictish ogham and Norse runic inscriptions, part of a Pictish symbol stone and the hooded figurine discussed below.

The whole of this fertile coastal area, along with the uplands to the west, is known as Cunningsburgh, formerly Coningburg, an Old Norse name meaning the king's fort, and it may be that one of the broch-sites, perhaps Mail itself, was the king's fort. Why should there have been a place here of such high status that the incoming Vikings coined a name for it? Fertile land is certainly a good reason, and the secure anchorage of Aith Voe is another, but what makes the area really special is the geology of the steep hillside to the south of Mail. Along the Catpund Burn are outcrops of steatite (soapstone), a soft and easily quarried rock that was in great demand for a wide range of equipment from fishermen's line-sinkers to kitchen bowls. Steatite was a valuable resource and control of the steatite industry would be an excellent economic basis for a royal power-base. The Norwegian Vikings who colonised Shetland in the later ninth century were accustomed to using steatite in their homeland, and taking over the Catpund steatite quarry and the Pictish royal stronghold would make good economic and political sense.

Present location

The Shetland Museum, Lerwick, Shetland.

References

Turner, V 1994 'The Mail stone: an incised Pictish figure from Mail, Cunningsburgh, Shetland', *Proc Soc Antiq Scot*, 124 (1994), 315–25.

Henderson, G & Henderson, I 2004 *The Art of the Picts*, 123. London: Thames & Hudson.

Ritchie, A 2003 'Paganism among the Picts and the conversion of Orkney', *in* Downes, J & Ritchie, A (eds) *Sea Change: Orkney and Northern Europe in the later Iron Age AD 300-800*, 3–10. Balgavies, Angus: The Pinkfoot Press.

The fearsome Rhynie man

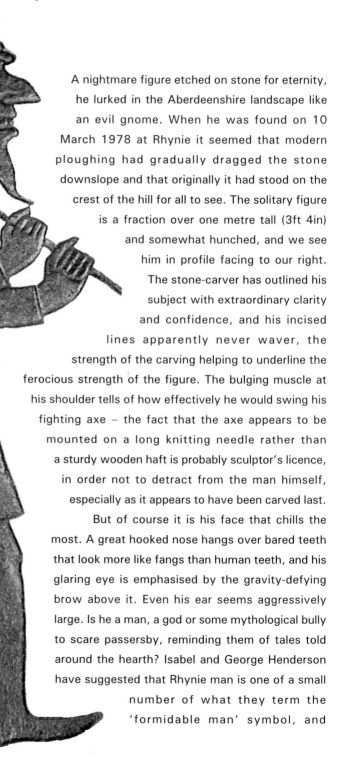

A nightmare figure etched on stone for eternity, he lurked in the Aberdeenshire landscape like an evil gnome. When he was found on 10 March 1978 at Rhynie it seemed that modern ploughing had gradually dragged the stone downslope and that originally it had stood on the crest of the hill for all to see. The solitary figure is a fraction over one metre tall (3ft 4in) and somewhat hunched, and we see him in profile facing to our right. The stone-carver has outlined his subject with extraordinary clarity and confidence, and his incised lines apparently never waver, the strength of the carving helping to underline the ferocious strength of the figure. The bulging muscle at his shoulder tells of how effectively he would swing his fighting axe – the fact that the axe appears to be mounted on a long knitting needle rather than a sturdy wooden haft is probably sculptor's licence, in order not to detract from the man himself, especially as it appears to have been carved last.

But of course it is his face that chills the most. A great hooked nose hangs over bared teeth that look more like fangs than human teeth, and his glaring eye is emphasised by the gravity-defying brow above it. Even his ear seems aggressively large. Is he a man, a god or some mythological bully to scare passersby, reminding them of tales told around the hearth? Isabel and George Henderson have suggested that Rhynie man is one of a small number of what they term the 'formidable man' symbol, and

8 *The Rhynie slab set up in Woodhill House* (© Tom & Sybil Gray Collection)

certainly the message that this carving conveys must have been instantly recognisable to a Pictish viewer. All the 'formidable man' symbols walk from left to right, unlike most hunting scenes that take place from right to left.

His short belted tunic has echoes of that worn by the Mail figure, but this time the skirt of the tunic has no extra seaming and there are clearly sleeves to the wrist. Some sort of headdress runs down to the middle of his back, or perhaps, as it follows the contour of his body, this is long hair on a man bald on top. He is often described as wearing leggings or pointed shoes but it is more likely that he is barefoot, because close-fitting leggings were impossible to achieve at this date and, had the carver intended to show shoes, there would be a line at the ankle.

Close to where Rhynie man stood originally, there still stands a symbol stone known as the Craw Stane, apparently in its original position and carved with two large symbols, the fish (a salmon) and the Pictish beast or elephant. This stone appears to be related to an archaeological site enclosed by two ditches that is only clearly visible as a cropmark from the air, but excavations are underway in an effort to clarify this interesting association of symbol stone with settlement. Several other symbol stones have been found in the vicinity and there can be little doubt that this was a centre of Pictish political power. If we could be sure that the Mail and Rhynie figures were associated with domestic settlements, we could justifiably speculate as to whether they had both been part of pagan shrines, focal points in everyday life.

Present location

In the foyer of Aberdeenshire Council's Woodhill House, Westburn Road, Aberdeen.

References

Shepherd, I A G & Shepherd, A N 1978 'An incised Pictish figure and a new symbol stone from Barflat, Rhynie, Gordon District', *Proc Soc Antiq Scot*, 109 (1977-7), 211–22.

Henderson, G & Henderson, I 2004 *The Art of the Picts*, 123. London: Thames & Hudson.

Gondek, M & Noble, G 2006 'Landscape with symbols', *British Archaeology*, March April 2006, 16–17.

The Lady of Cadboll

Many Pictish carved stones have been moved, modified or re-used but the record for such vicissitudes must surely be held by the magnificent Hilton of Cadboll cross-slab. It has been appreciated as a work of art since it was first published and illustrated by an antiquarian named Charles Cordiner, yet by then the slab had not merely been felled but badly mutilated. The cross-face had been chipped off in order to convert it into a graveslab with the inscription:

> He that lives well does well
> Sayeth Solomon the wise
> Here lies Alexander Duff
> and his three wives 1676

Adding insult to injury, the stone was never used for Duff's grave, perhaps because it proved too massive to transport to Fearn where he was buried. It must have been raised sufficiently for Charles Cordiner to see the underside with its intact carving, but he appears to have appreciated the need to protect the carving by leaving it face down. Around 1811 the stone was placed in a shed on site, until in the late 19th century it was taken to Invergordon Castle and set upright into a modern base beside the driveway. In 1921 Captain Macleod of Invergordon sent the great cross-slab to the British Museum, but after considerable public protest in Scotland it was returned north to the Museum of Antiquities in Edinburgh (now the Museum of Scotland).

This superb monument has three panels of decoration enclosed within a wide border of beautifully scrolling vines, each scroll inhabited by a bird. With huge symbols above and a carpet of spirals below, the central hunting scene draws the eye as if through a window into a vanished Pictish world. There is much going on here, but the most important figure is clearly the lady facing sideways on her horse and announced by her trumpeters. Women rarely appear on Pictish sculpture, where the narrative is generally concerned with male warriors, huntsmen and clerics, and it is hard to judge whether she is a local aristocrat, a rendering of a figure from classical literature (the Hendersons suggest the Queen of Carthage), the Celtic goddess Epona or a depiction of the Virgin Mary. The folds of her robe appear to be held at the chest by what was identified by Robert Stevenson as a massive penannular brooch, though it has also been

9 *The Hilton of Cadboll cross-slab* (drawing and copyright by Ian G Scott)

surface
lost

10 *The hunting scene* (drawing and copyright by Ian G Scott)

Ian G Scott explains why a cross-slab should be drawn.

Even when we can afford laser scans and extensive photographic recording, there is always a need for a measured drawing which summarizes what can be verified by observation from all sources. It is the graphic extension and completion of any written description.

How to represent what can be seen poses difficult choices. Our subjects have a third dimension, and the modelling of the shapes is seldom sharp and clear after centuries of exposure. Until recently, only ink applied in dots (stipple) answered the problems of reproduction and archive of the original, as well as being capable of suggesting form, depth and edges of the modelling. Fig 9 uses a stipple drawing on a grey background that has been scraped to reveal the white paper and thus suggest the modelling. Some details have been tentatively enhanced. For the detail of the hunting panel (Fig 10), I have tried a pencil original, quickly photocopied before it inevitably smudges with handling. This could be developed with an even gradation of tone, like a photograph, an effect not readily possible with ink. I have indicated by crossed lines where superficial layers have laminated and disappeared.

interpreted, less convincingly, as a falcon's perch. She has a companion behind her, whose horse is visible as a second outline to her own and whose face is glimpsed in profile behind her elaborately dressed hair. The entire panel is in praise of her royal status, from her bodyguard and musicians to the hunters indulging in the favourite pastime of her court. Do the mirror and comb symbols signify both her status and her gender?

The chapel at Hilton of Cadboll was built in the 12th century on a site of much older ecclesiastical significance, as the cross-slab implies. Excavations beside the chapel in 1998 discovered thousands of fragments from the 17th-century destruction of the cross-face, and more were retrieved in 2001, when to everyone's delight the original lower portion of the slab was found about 6m beyond the west gable of the chapel. This supplied not only most of the rest of the back of the slab but also a first exciting glimpse of the missing cross-face, which had a stepped base to the cross and figures with animals on either side. It will be an enormous task to reconstruct the layout of the rest of the cross-face from the surviving fragments. There has been no full treatment in print of this outstanding monument, but the new discoveries at Hilton of Cadboll have prompted a major project that will help to fill this gap in our understanding of Easter Ross in Pictish times.

Present location

The larger part of the stone is in the Museum of Scotland in Edinburgh, and the lower portion is in the Memorial Hall at Balintore, Easter Ross. The sculptor, Barry Grove, has created an imaginative reconstruction of the cross-slab, which was completed in 2005 and stands close to the chapel site at Hilton of Cadboll (NH 87317687).

References

Cordiner, C 1780 *Antiquities and Scenery of the North of Britain*, 66. London.

Henderson, G & Henderson, I 2004 *The Art of the Picts*, 136. London: Thames & Hudson.

James, H, Henderson, I, Foster, S M & Jones, S forthcoming *A Fragmented Masterpiece: recovering the biography of the Hilton of Cadboll Pictish cross-slab. Excavations at Hilton of Cadboll chapel, Highland, from 1998 to 2003*.

Stevenson, R B K 1959 'The Inchyra stone and other unpublished Early Christian monuments', *Proc Soc Antiq Scot*, 92 (1958-9), 33–55.

11 *The back of the Aberlemno Churchyard cross-slab* (© Tom & Sybil Gray Collection)

26

Aberlemno: the story of a battle

With its consummate artistry this cross-slab is a startling sight in the churchyard at Aberlemno in Angus. A thick slab of the local sandstone of Strathmore was dressed to an elegant tapering form with a gabled top, and the cross-face was further dressed to allow the Christian cross to stand out 100mm from its background. The decoration of that background shows to perfection the Pictish love of a subtle asymmetry that is not immediately apparent: the two beasts flanking the top arm of the cross look identical at first glance, but they are not, and the three animals that spiral up the left side of the cross-shaft appear to create a repeating pattern but there are small and deliberate divergences. Even the pair of sea-horses dancing their *pas de deux* are not identical.

Standing 2.3m high and 1.3m wide at the base, the back of the slab presented the sculptor with a broad blank canvas on which to work. His brief had clearly been quite specific, to celebrate the military might of the Picts. Within a frame that turns into two animals with jaws agape at the top, an epic battle takes place, defined by the two great symbols that hang above: a notched rectangle with Z-rod and a triple disc that seems to act as a link with the scene below. The hole that pierces the stone through one leg of the rectangle is a mystery and must relate to some episode in its later history. Both symbols and battle scene are carved in a combination of low relief and incision, the latter sometimes used as a device to convey perspective, as for instance with the spear held by the horseman middle right.

The story of the battle is told like a strip cartoon in three registers and it is full of movement. The two forces of warriors are easily distinguished: those on the right wear helmets with prominent nose-guards, while those on the left are bare-headed with shoulder-length tresses. At the top a horseman brandishing his sword chases another horseman who, intent on flight, has abandoned his round shield and sword. Below, three ranks of foot-soldiers face an enemy horseman and they present a succinct vignette of battle tactics. The leading foot-soldier carries his shield before him as protection against the horseman's spear and has his sword raised ready to strike. Shield hanging free, the second warrior uses both hands to brace his spear against the oncoming horse, neatly covering the man in front, and the third warrior marches with spear at rest until his turn

12 *The front of the cross-slab in 1968*
(© Audrey S Henshall)

comes to engage with the enemy. The two horsemen in the bottom row are poised to hurl their spears, the one on the right reining in his horse to steady him and his opponent's horse running free as his raises his shield in his left hand. The outcome of the battle is shown by the vanquished warlord lying dead on the field of battle, prey to a carrion bird, still wearing his helmet and mail tunic. The sculptor has used the common device of showing status by making the dead warrior larger than life.

Battle scenes are very rare in Pictish art and there must be an element of doubt over whether the Aberlemno battle depicts an historical battle or simply military might. Is it just co-incidence that the best-known Pictish battle took place just 10 km to the south at Dunnichen in AD 685? This was the battle described by Bede in 731 between the Picts and the Northumbrians, which put an end to English occupation of southern Pictland, and Leslie Alcock has suggested that the occasion for carving the stone may have been the publication of Bede's manuscript. A date in the third or fourth decade of the 8th century would certainly fit the art style of the cross-slab.

Present location

In the churchyard at Aberlemno, Angus.

References

Chalmers, P 1848 *The Ancient Sculptured Monuments of the County of Angus*, 8. Edinburgh: Bannatyne Club.

Alcock, L 1993 'Image and icon in Pictish sculpture', *in* Spearman, R M & Higgitt, J (eds) *The Age of Migrating Ideas: Early Medieval Art in Northern Britain and Ireland*, 230–6. Stroud: Alan Sutton Publishing.

Cruickshank, G D R 2000 'The battle of Dunnichen and the Aberlemno battle-scene', *in* Cowan, E J & McDonald, R A (eds) *Alba: Celtic Scotland in the Middle Ages*, 69–87. East Linton, East Lothian: The Tuckwell Press.

Fraser, J 2002 *The Battle of Dunnichen 685*. Stroud: Tempus Publishing Ltd.

The monks of Papil

The most remarkable aspect of this monkish scene from Papil in Shetland is that each face is different. These are not blandly stylized clerics but, despite their uniform hooded cloaks, carefully depicted individuals. This is particularly true of the figure on horseback, his cloak bunched about him and his face clearly that of an old man with a heavy fold of flesh from nose to jaw. The sculptor is evoking a scene and characters familiar to his audience and specified by his patron. Charles Thomas suggested that it shows Christianity being brought over the waves of the sea to Shetland. Each of the monks on foot has a crooked staff, and the one at the rear of the procession has a book satchel over his shoulder, all very appropriate for missionaries. But who is the elderly monk on horseback? He was surely a saint well-known and long-venerated by the eighth century when this slab was carved, but there are no historical records to give us any hint of his identity. He may have led an Irish mission to the pagan Shetlanders, or he may have come with all the authority of the Roman Church from the court of the Pictish high-king. Part of a graveslab incised with an Irish

13 *The Monks Stone* (© The Shetland Museum)

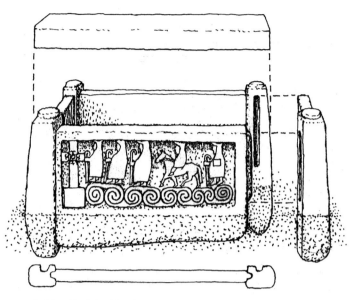

14 *A reconstructed slab-built shrine* (drawing and copyright by Ian G Scott)

type of interlace cross was found at the same time as this slab and may perhaps suggest a western connection.

The sculptor employed a clever combination of low relief, achieved by pecking away the background, and incision for details such as the satchel and its straps, the reins and bridle, and eyes and fingers. He must have been cross with himself for the mistake he made with the line of spirals, apparently carved freehand without planning, for he started at the left-hand end and ran out of space towards the right. The free-standing cross to which the monks process is a symbol of Christianity rather than a reflection of any such cross existing at the time in Shetland. The horse can be identified as a native Shetland pony, larger than those of today, which were bred small in the 19th century to work in coal mines.

Pleasing to the eye both for the simplicity of its workmanship and for the coherence of the scene, this slab was designed to be one of the long sides of a rectangular box-shrine. It was found in April 1943 during grave-digging in the kirkyard of St Laurence's at Papil in Shetland. Papil is in West Burra, which with East Burra forms a group of elongated islands separated from the west coast of the south mainland of Shetland by the steep-sided fjord aptly named Clift Sound. The fine-grained sandstone for the slab came from the mainland, probably by way of the little bay of May Wick some 6km to the south of Papil. The other three sides of the shrine have yet to be found, but grooved corner-posts survive. The slab is 1m long and 0.57m high, and thus the complete shrine would have been quite substantial. It would have stood within the early church and was probably designed to hold relics of a saint, perhaps the elderly monk shown riding a horse.

The kirkyard at Papil has yielded parts of no fewer than three box-shrines, more than anywhere else in Scotland, and, just south of West Burra, St Ninian's Isle can boast another two. Yet none has been found in Orkney, nor indeed in mainland Scotland north of the Dornoch Firth. This suggests a special role for the early church at Papil, most probably as the focus of a monastery, and the place name Papil represents a Norse naming of a site known to them to be associated with priests.

The dedication of the church to St Laurence is unlikely to date before the 12th century, when a steeple kirk was built at Papil. Steeple kirk is the term used in Orkney and Shetland for churches with tall round towers, of which the sole survivor is St Magnus' Church, Egilsay, in Orkney. There were at least three such churches in Shetland at Papil, at Ireland south of May Wick in mainland and Tingwall north of Scalloway, and they were important churches, at Papil reflecting the status of the earlier church and at Tingwall marking the location of the Norse ting or parliament. Whether the saint celebrated at Papil was the Laurence who was martyred at Rome in AD 258 (beloved by the Norsemen for his grisly end roasted on a gridiron) or the Laurence who accompanied St Augustine to Canterbury and died in 619, he is not likely to be the horse-borne monk of the earlier Papil shrine.

Present location

The Shetland Museum, Lerwick, Shetland.

References

Moar, Peter and Stewart, John 1944 'Newly discovered sculptured stones from Papil, Shetland', *Proc Soc Antiq Scot*, 78 (1943-4), 91–9.

Thomas, Charles 1973 'Sculptured stones and crosses from St. Ninian's Isle and Papil', *in* Small, A, Thomas, C & Wilson, D M *St. Ninian's Isle and its treasure*, 8–44. Oxford: Oxford University Press.

Holy thrones at Fowlis Wester

This is a curious cross-slab, on which extraordinarily elaborate detail on the carved face contrasts with the undressed chunkiness of the rest of the stone. It was perhaps unfinished, for there has been natural flaking of the stone towards the bottom right, and the carving in that area seems to have been abandoned. The sculptor's disappointment can barely be imagined, and yet as a result his work has survived in far better condition than if it had been finished and exposed to the elements in the churchyard.

The stone was found during restoration of the 13th-century church in the village of Fowlis Wester in Perthshire in about 1931 by J Jeffrey Waddell. The old harling was stripped off the north wall of the church, and near the base of the wall Waddell noticed an abnormally long stone. He wrote 'I managed to get my hand under it – it seemed to be just clay-built – so far as to feel what I suspected were carvings. We got the stone out without damaging it'. The stone is 1.6m high, 0.8m wide tapering to 0.5m at the top and about 0.3m thick, but somewhat triangular in profile. It seems odd that the sculptor expended such effort on the stone before trimming it into the normal slab flat on both sides – could it have been intended for display within the earlier 9th-century church, built upright into its east wall?

The ringed cross is entirely filled with interlace, and its base has an inner panel of spirals surrounded by fret pattern. The cross is clearly the most important element of the design, and yet the eye is drawn to the seated figures on either side of the shaft of the cross. To the right the monk is seated on a decorated chair with a spiral terminal, and there is an attendant with long curled hair and hands clasped across the chest behind him. To the left, the monk is seated on what can only be described as a throne, highly decorated and with an animal head at the top of the back of the chair. In both cases the slippered feet of the monks rest upon footstools, and their robes are elaborately embroidered with decorative bands at the hem. That these robes are hooded can be seen by the triangular shapes at the nape of the neck, which represent hoods thrown back off the head. Similar hooded robes and slippers are worn by the two monks standing on the left-hand side of the cross-base.

5 *The cross-slab inside the church at Fowlis Wester (with a later medieval slab in the right foreground)*
© Tom & Sybil Gray Collection)

16 *St Paul on his throne-like chair* (© Tom & Sybil Gray Collection)

A closer look at the enthroned cleric on the left reveals that he is tonsured (his hair has been trimmed into an open crown around his head). In front of him is a long-stemmed plant or tree with nine buds or perhaps more likely a date palm. Behind him is a plant or tree with both fruit and leaves: four fruit and six leaves, and here the fruit may be gourds. The grandeur of his throne proclaims his authority: high-backed and terminating in a beast's head with a long snout, with a curving side-panel decorated with key-pattern. Did the sculptor have in mind a wooden chair or a carved stone chair?

These two seated figures can be recognised as the desert saints of the 4th century AD, Paul and Anthony. Here St Paul is symbolised by a date palm and St Anthony by the Heavenly Vision, and they appear on other Pictish stones at St Vigeans in Angus, Dunfallandy in Perthshire and Nigg in Ross and Cromarty, though without the decorative detail of Fowlis Wester. There is also imagery from the Old Testament at Fowlis Wester, for the two scenes at the top of the stone show first the whale swallowing Jonah, who has dropped his Pictish sword and shield, and then the whale regurgitating Jonah unharmed. This stone is a fine example of Christian iconography presented with loving Pictish embellishment.

Present location

Inside the church at Fowlis Wester in Perthshire.

References

Waddell, J Jeffrey 1932 'Cross-slabs recently discovered at Fowlis Wester and Millport', *Proc Soc Antiq Scot*, 66 (1931-2), 409–12.

Musicians at the Tower of Lethendy

Until 1969, archaeologists had no idea that there was a fragment of Pictish sculpture built into a late medieval tower-house at Lethendy, near Blairgowrie in Perthshire. Ian Fisher of the Royal Commission on the Ancient and Historical Monuments of Scotland was the first to record it and to recognise its importance, particularly for studies of early music in Scotland. The slab is 1.35m high, 0.36m wide and 0.13m thick, quite a narrow cross-slab like some of those at Meigle in Perthshire.

Beneath and perhaps protected by an angel with half-spread wings, a pair of clerics with large and remarkably bland faces sit side-by-side on a bench, their feet quite bare, like

17 *The back of the Tower of Lethendy cross-slab with seated clerics and musicians*
(© Tom & Sybil Gray Collection)

18 *Detail of the panel with musicians* (© Tom & Sybil Gray Collection)

those of the angel. Each wears a voluminous robe gathered over a tunic with decorated hem, perhaps embroidered or trimmed with patterned braid, and the sculptor has been careful to show a different pattern on each robe. The left-hand cleric carries a rectangular object apparently by a handle, and it is heavy enough, or precious enough, to require a second hand to support it from below. It may be an illustrated gospel-book, but the handle implies that this may be a box reliquary. His companion carries a short rod in his right hand and what may be a hand-bell in his left.

In a separate framed panel at the foot of the stone is a unique scene with two musicians in action and a small pet dog. The musicians' robes are belted so as to leave their arms free to play the harp and the triple pipe, and between them a third instrument, probably a barrel-shaped drum, may have hung on a strap round the piper's neck. Clearly wearing a collar, the dog is a stocky animal with a long head, like a modern Welsh corgi, and the skeleton of just such a dog was excavated along with its mistress in a grave dating to about AD 800 at Machrins in the island of Colonsay. The presence of the dog in this minstrel scene is usually explained as a conflation of two images of the biblical David: David the musician and David the shepherd. But it must be admitted that the animal could equally well be a pig.

The harp is a special Pictish type which is triangular in shape, thus adding both strength to the frame and extra strings for a clearer sound and an extended range of notes. The frame would be made of wood and the strings of horse-hair or animal gut. Here, as on the Dupplin Cross, the sculptor has been at pains to show the harpist's fingers on the strings. John Purser believes that the triple pipe would have sounded like the bagpipes, despite the lack of a bag, and that the drum would have had a low pitch. This 10th-century ensemble would have been capable of a wide range of music.

19 *The harpist on the right-hand side-panel of the Dupplin Cross* (drawing by Ian G Scott; Crown Copyright: Historic Scotland)

When the stone was removed from the staircase and conserved in 2001, the cross-face was revealed, along with the neatly rounded top of the slab. Unexpectedly the shaft of the cross itself and the central part of the scene below have been gouged out at some time to form a shallow trough, and thus the re-use of the slab as a lintel in the staircase of the tower-house was not the first occasion on which it had been re-used. There are also smooth rounded hollows along the edges where people have sharpened their knives. To the left of where the shaft of the cross should be, there is key pattern above a human figure in profile facing towards the shaft, while on the right is more key pattern, a double knot of double ribbon and another collared animal. Again it looks like a dog with a high curled tail, but a far more ferocious dog with bared teeth and a corrugated snout. The collars on these two animals are unique in Pictish sculpture and may have a significance of their own.

Present location

In the entrance hall at Tower of Lethendy, Perthshire (privately owned).

References

Fisher, I & Greenhill, F A 1972 'Two unrecorded carved stones at Tower of Lethendy, Perthshire', *Proc Soc Antiq Scot*, 104 (1972-4), 238–41.

Purser, John 1992 *Scotland's Music*. Edinburgh: Mainstream Publishing.

Trench-Jellicoe, Ross 1997 'Pictish and related harps: their form and decoration', *in* Henry, David (ed) *The worm, the germ and the thorn: Pictish and related studies presented to Isabel Henderson*, 159–72. Balgavies, Angus: The Pinkfoot Press.

20 *The collared hound on the cross-face (here shown horizontally)* (© Tom & Sybil Gray Collection)

21 *The Bullion stone* (© Tom & Sybil Gray Collection)

Bullion: sorry tale or caricature?

This extraordinary image of human frailty is unique amongst the great corpus of Pictish sculpture. As his horse plods patiently uphill, the elderly rider with his bald head and rampant beard drinks from an overlarge horn. His bulbous nose and rounded belly suggest that this is a favoured pastime, and his shield hangs on the wrong side to show his confusion. The large bird's head that decorates the tip of the horn seems to be watching him drink. Is this a caricature of a well-known local figure or a graphic rendering of a sorry tale to warn the passerby of the dangers of drinking too much heather ale? That he has come down in the world is clear from his mount. As Robert Beck a veterinary surgeon, has observed, 'This is not a poor illustration of a horse. On the contrary, the portrayal is excellent, but of a very poor horse. The animal has been a fine specimen ... but is now aged and infirm'.

The stone was found in 1934 during roadworks on the western outskirts of Dundee at Bullion near Invergowrie. It lay buried on the crest of a small ridge less than a kilometre from the shore of the Firth of Tay and had perhaps stood beside an early trackway, like a roadside billboard of modern times. Though broken, the sandstone slab is still almost two metres high, and there is nothing carved on the other side. The sculptor used the technique of low relief to create his image within a panel the lower edge of which became the hillside, while the drinking horn extends beyond the frame, almost giving the bird a life of its own. Most of the details are incised, such as the shield and its strap, though some are so deeply incised as to give the impression of relief – the old man's fleshy ear, for example, and the horse's mane. Oddly there is little sign of a saddle cloth, and the left arm must be hidden behind the right, for surely both would be needed to hold the horn, even in its apparently half-empty state.

The character of this slab is quite different from the two cross-slabs found close to the old parish church in the village of Invergowrie, which were memorial stones. The wry humour of the Bullion figure makes it stand alone, in much the same way as the Mail and Rhynie men, and again we must regret the loss of Pictish mythology and folk-tales that might have provided answers to the identity of these distinctive figures. There are no other certain drinking horns in Pictish sculpture, though there are blast-horns, and a decorative silver mounting for the mouth of a blast-horn of Anglo-Saxon origin was found in the Pictish fort at Burghead in Moray. In early medieval Irish literature, decorated drinking horns are a mark of social status that reflect their owner's ability to dispense essential hospitality, and some horns were named and became famous. The Bullion horn may have been as well known to the Pictish tribes of the Tay as its ale-quaffing owner.

Present location

In the Museum of Scotland, Chambers Street, Edinburgh.

References

Beck, R 1992 *Scotland's Native Horse: its history, breeding and survival*, 148. Wigton: G C Book Publishers Ltd.

Neuman de Vegvar, Carol 1995 'Drinking horns in Ireland and Wales: documentary sources', *in* Bourke, C (ed) *From the Isles of the North: Early Medieval Art in Ireland and Britain*, 81–7. Belfast: HMSO.

Stevenson, R B K 1959 'The Inchyra Stone and some other unpublished Early Christian monuments', *Proc Soc Antiq Scot*, 92 (1958-9), 33–55.

An archer at St Vigeans

22 *The archer and his prey* (© Tom & Sybil Gray Collection)

The back of this fine cross-slab is full of interest, not least the scene at the foot of the carved panel. An archer kneels on one knee ready to fire off an arrow at an approaching boar. For maximum effect the sculptor has condensed the scene in such a way that we can admire not only the new technology of the archer's cross-bow but also the healthy young boar angrily scratching the ground, hackles raised, head down and tusks at the ready. In reality of course the archer would have been felled by the boar's onslaught, even if he had got his bow horizontal and ready to fire in time, but the sculptor's audience understands that there is some artistic license here. This image of the crouching archer and boar appears on other stones (eg Meigle no 10 and Shandwick) and is an allusion to a story

now lost but familiar to the Picts. Indeed the Pictish observer might well have known the name of the archer as well as the end of the story.

The bow is easily identified as a cross-bow rather than a longbow, for there is no forward hand on the bow, and the shaft of the arrow can be seen lying along the bow-stock. No certain trace of cross-bows has been found in Scotland earlier than Pictish times, though the longbow has an ancient pedigree stretching back some three thousand years before. The archer wears a short tunic beneath a hooded cloak short enough to leave his arms free and to allow him to crouch without an excess of material around his legs. His cloak has such an air of rigidity about it that it may have been made of leather, which would also be suitably waterproof, though Elizabeth Sutherland has suggested that it might be an animal skin worn for disguise.

Looking at the carvings above the archer scene, it is clear that the sculptor was good with figures but not so good with abstract designs. The double disc and Z-rod symbol has fairly rudimentary interlace filling the discs, while the decoration of the crescent symbol can only be described as inept. The mirror and comb to the right of the crescent are efficient but no more. But the myriad creatures below are superb. A bear pads

23 *The back of the Drosten cross-slab*
(© Tom & Sybil Gray Collection)

along; a deer suckles her kid; below her an oversized hybrid goat struts, while before him a bird of prey feasts on a fish, and an unfortunate animal is squashed into the design only by dint of turning its head to fit between the goat's horn and the bear's front paws.

This stone is one of a fascinating collection of carved stones at St Vigeans, near Arbroath in Angus. The tiny village of St Vigeans is dominated by a steep natural mound on which the parish church was built and dedicated to a 7th-century Irish saint, St Fechin (Vigianus in Latin). The present church was restored in the 1870s and many of the Early Christian carved stones were found built into the walls of the old church. There are cross-slabs, recumbent grave-slabs and even a free-standing cross. The stone displaying our archer and his boar is known as the Drosten Stone, because it bears an important inscription which includes the Pictish personal name Drosten and which allows the stone to be dated. Thomas Clancy has argued that the inscription is in Irish Gaelic and reads 'Drosten, in the time of Uoret, and Forcus'. The reference to Uoret is to a Pictish king, Uurad son of Bargoit, who reigned from AD 839 to 842. Whether the stone commemorates the death of an aristocratic Pict named Drosten, or whether Drosten was the respected sculptor of the cross-slab, we shall probably never know.

Present location

The Drosten Stone is cross-slab no 1 in the Historic Scotland museum at St Vigeans on the north-west outskirts of Arbroath, Angus.

References

Clancy, Thomas Owen 1993 'The Drosten Stone: a new reading', *Proc Soc Antiq Scot*, 123 (1993), 345–53.

Sutherland, Elizabeth 1994 *In Search of the Picts*, 183. London: Constable & Company Ltd.

24 *The huntsmen on the back of the Kirriemuir cross-slab* (© Tom & Sybil Gray Collection)

The horsemen of Kirriemuir

All across Scotland in the late 18th century there was a spate of church-building, demolishing sometimes very fine medieval churches in the march of progress. At Kirriemuir in Angus in 1787, the demolition led to the discovery of early Christian carved stones that had been built into the foundations of the medieval church. The stones were taken to a new cemetery on the flank of the Hill of Kirriemuir and set upright there, and eventually, in the 20th century, they were placed in a lean-to shelter within the cemetery. The one stone that remained in the kirkyard had no figures or symbols other than the Christian cross and was clearly re-used, probably more than once, as a gravestone. Today, thankfully, they are all in the care of Angus Museums Service in Forfar. Such a history is common, from stones being trimmed as building slabs to their removal to another site or even another part of Scotland.

From the Hill of Kirriemuir is visible the wide expanse of fertile Strathmore, the heart of 8th- and 9th-century Pictland, and the large number of carved stones at Kirriemuir implies that there were powerful patrons being buried here. There are seventeen complete or fragmentary cross-slabs, with a range of well-executed interlace designs, and four bear human figures. The local sculptors appear to have been quite competent at interlace, probably following a book of patterns, but they were curiously inept in their renderings of humans and animals.

The cross-slab illustrated here is 1.13m high and has a cross on one face, flanked at the top by angels, on the left side of the shaft by a foot soldier and on the right by three hounds, a stag and a bird of prey. The other face is decorated by a single figural panel telling two different stories. In the lower part is a mounted huntsman closing in on the stag for a kill, and the stag's rump has a hound's teeth firmly fastened on it, all three animals carved to convey great speed. This has been described as 'one of the most spirited hunting scenes of the whole Pictish series'. But dominating the panel is a stately horseborne warrior accompanied by a double disc and Z-rod symbol that may denote his status – and an ogham inscription along one side of the slab may, if only we could read it, give his name. Whoever he is, the carving barely does him credit. His horse has the front legs of a pantomime horse, and the stone carver was clearly at a loss as to how to depict arms. Yet there are lots of interesting details, such as

25 *The cross-face with angels, foot soldier, stag and hounds*
(drawing by John Borland; Crown Copyright: RCAHMS)

the hilt and guard of the sword that projects from his left-hand side, the two layers of saddle-cloth on which he sits and his garments. He appears to be wearing a short pleated tunic, gartered trousers and a curiously corrugated shoulder-cape, which could be a draped plaid, but the whole outfit may be a poor copy of some more classical image.

The faces of the two warriors are quite different, and they were evidently not intended to show the same man in two roles. This is an off-the-shelf gravestone to suit any Pict wealthy enough to barter for it, and the images are stereotypes of the heroic life.

Present location

Meffan Museum and Gallery, 20 West High Street, Forfar.

Reference

Royal Commission on the Ancient and Historical Monuments of Scotland 2003 *Early Medieval Sculpture in Angus Council Museums*, Kirriemuir 2. RCAHMS Broadsheet 11.

A fine face from Golspie

A gardener in Golspie on the east coast of Sutherland was rewarded for her efforts one day in June 1974 by the discovery of a unique Pictish dress-pin. It had been lost, perhaps some time in the 7th or 8th century AD, as a result of a violent mishap, for the shaft of the pin is bent and broken. What makes it unique is the face that decorates its flat head. It is a male face, for it has a moustache and a beard sufficiently luxuriant to be plaited beneath the chin. His ears protrude in such a way as to make them an intentionally obvious feature, and his eyes are large and oval. Above them his forehead is heavily creased by three horizontal lines as if to convey great surprise – or could they represent painted or tattooed lines?

The pin was cast in bronze in a two-piece clay mould, and the surface of the face was then gilded. It was worn often enough for much of the gilding to have vanished except in the crevices, and it was probably used to fasten a cloak. The back of the head is quite plain, but the collar beneath the head extends all round. Allowing for the broken shaft, the intact pin might have been about 80mm long, the shaft 3.5mm in diameter and the head 15mm wide, quite a small item of costly jewellery perhaps more appropriate to a woman or child than a man.

Is this the face of a particular Pict or is it an artistic stereotype? The lines on the forehead seem to be the most notable aspect of the design, and there is just one other object bearing human faces with furrowed brows: a small elongated pebble, 143mm long, from Portsoy on the southern shore of the Moray Firth (now in the British Museum). One end of the pebble is domed and bears an incised face with eyes closed, five lines on its forehead and carefully delineated ears, while at the other end a slightly smaller face has four lines and no ears and seems to gaze up towards the first face.

26 *The Golspie pin* (© Trustees of the National Museums of Scotland)

27 *The Portsoy pebble* (drawing by Ian G Scott; Crown Copyright: RCAHMS)

Between them are a fish (and there is another fish on the other side of the pebble), a cross and four rudimentary crescents. It has been suggested that the two faces represent life and death, but the differences between them might rather imply something to do with hearing and sight, like two of the three monkeys of fable, 'hear no evil' and 'see no evil'. It is clearly an object of special and perhaps ritual significance – but not, as often described, the whetstone from a royal sceptre. The furrowed brows of the Portsoy faces suggest that the face on the Golspie pin had a special significance for its wearer, perhaps related to Pictish mythology. The fish is reminiscent of the face-cross from Riasg Buidhe.

The fertile coastal strip on either side of Golspie was well populated in Pictish times, as demonstrated by the fifteen symbol stones that have been found within a radius of 11km. Some could afford to commission carved stones and fine dress ornaments. Clothes were loose rather than tailored in a modern sense, and pins and brooches were essential items to hold garments together, not just to decorate them – cloaks in particular needed to be pinned at the shoulder. Pins carved of bone would suffice for most of the population, but for the wealthy and powerful brooches and pins of bronze, silver and gold were symbols of their social status in the community as well as practical items. The huge brooch worn by the Hilton of Cadboll lady is a clear example of power-dressing.

Present location

Museum of Scotland, Chambers Street, Edinburgh.

References

Close-Brooks, Joanna 1975 'A Pictish pin from Golspie, Sutherland', *Proc Soc Antiq Scot*, 106 (1974-5), 208–10.

Ritchie, A 2005 'Clothing among the Picts', *Costume*, 39 (2005), 28–42.

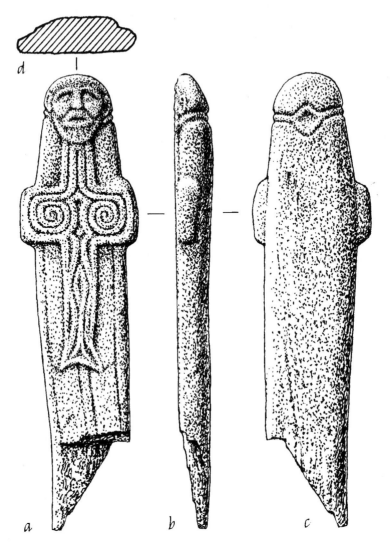

28 *Front, side and back of the Riasg Buidhe face-cross* (drawing by Ian G Scott; Crown Copyright: RCAHMS)

The face-cross from Riasg Buidhe

In a tranquil glade in the gardens of Colonsay House stands a quite remarkable cross-slab. The stone has been dressed and carved in such a way that from behind it looks like a cloaked figure with the hood folded back into a neat triangle at the nape of the neck, while the front is a crucifixion with a difference. A strong but gentle face gazes out, framed by prominent ears and a trimmed beard, atop a stylized body that merges partly with the cross. The arms of the cross are filled with thickly coiled spirals, and the same thick mouldings suggest legs above the hint of a fishtail. The two lines below give the effect of the wooden shaft to which the body was nailed.

This is a very clever and potent image. The fish was one of the earliest symbols of Christ, because the Greek word for fish, *ichthys*, consists of the initials of the words for 'Jesus Christ, Son of God, Saviour'. Here the fish symbol is combined not only with the symbol of the cross but with the crucifixion itself. It is the only face-cross in Scotland, but there are a few examples in Ireland, though none with comparable decorative quality. Ultimately of eastern Mediterranean origin, it is likely that the idea for such a cross-slab came to Colonsay with Irish monks in the 7th or 8th century. Although it stands quite appropriately beside Tobar Odhráin, St Oran's Well, this was not its original location, for it was brought here sometime before 1870 from the east side of the island. Riasg Buidhe is about 2km to the south-east of Colonsay House, and there are slight traces still of the ancient burial ground in which the face-cross once stood outside the east end of a small chapel. The base of the slab is broken and it probably stood little more than a metre above the turf as a grave-marker. Perhaps it marked the grave of an erudite and well-travelled Irish monk.

Throughout the 6th to 8th centuries, the western seaways of Scotland bore the skin-covered curraghs of many Irish monks, some seeking to found monasteries and hermitages, some to join existing communities and others on their way north to Orkney, Shetland, the Faeroes and Iceland. Some are known by name from written sources or from their gravestones — Cormac, Donnan, Colgu, Eogan — but many more remain anonymous. The Riasg Buidhe face-cross may commemorate one of these. The monks were not alone on the seaways, for there were also merchants bringing wine and olive oil from France and spices from the eastern Mediterranean, and a side-effect of the trade was the inevitable pirates, soon to be outdone by the real professionals, the Vikings. Raids on monasteries and secular communities in western Scotland by Norwegian Vikings are recorded from AD 795 onwards and may well have begun earlier.

29 *The cross in its present setting at Colonsay House* (© Graham Ritchie)

Present location

In the gardens of Colonsay House, Colonsay, Argyll.

References

Fisher, Ian 2001 *Early Medieval Sculpture in the West Highlands and Islands*. Edinburgh: RCAHMS/Society of Antiquaries of Scotland.

Loder, John de Vere 1935 *Colonsay and Oronsay in the Isles of Argyll: their history, flora, fauna and topography*. Edinburgh: Oliver & Boyd.

RCAHMS 1984 *Argyll: an inventory of the monuments, vol 5, Islay, Jura, Colonsay and Oronsay*, no 389. Edinburgh: HMSO.

A trio of warlords from Birsay

In 1935, excavations on the Brough of Birsay in Orkney revealed fragments of a carved stone slab. It had been broken up so thoroughly that its destruction must have been a deliberate act, though none of the carving had been defaced. The slab must originally have been at least 1.8m high, and it bears a unique vignette in low relief of three warlords and four Pictish symbols 'flying above their heads like standards'. The symbols are those known to us (but not to the Picts) as the disc with notched rectangle, the crescent and V-rod, the Pictish beast and the eagle. The analogy with standards belongs to Isabel and George Henderson, who emphasise that symbols, and here that includes the warrior group, should be understood as 'images of effective authority'. Orkney was part of the Pictish kingdom and had its own local ruler, and this image of ceremonial military might represented both levels of ruling authority.

Approached from the sea, the Brough presents cliffs up to 46m high against the mighty waves of the Atlantic, but it slopes down almost to sea level on its landward side. It has yet to be determined whether this tidal island was still attached to the Point of Buckquoy in Pictish and Norse times, but, island or promontory, it was an ideal location for a chieftain's residence. Excavations have revealed traces of the houses and fine metalworking activities of the Pictish settlement, and many of the Norse buildings are visible as low walling. The symbol stone reflects the importance of the place in Pictish times, and the fact that it was taken over by Norsemen early in the Viking colonisation of Orkney underlines that pre-eminence. Nothing could make a clearer statement of Norse supremacy than commandeering the indigenous seat of power – and smashing the monument that was a visual reminder of a Pictish past.

The sculptor has used an effective combination of incision and low relief to depict the three warriors and yet overall his repertoire seems quite limited. All the large objects have a double outline (disc, crescent and shields) and all the abstract decoration consists of curls (disc, crescent and leader's shield). What survives of the eagle's feathers is stiffly stylised, yet the outline of the beast is plump and fluid. The slab is uncluttered, unlike the crowded appearance of Pictish cross-slabs, and this is true of all the Orcadian symbol stones, for there are no large ornamented cross-slabs. There is a clear hierarchy between the figures,

30 *Drawing and part reconstruction of the Brough of Birsay slab by Ian G Scott* (Crown Copyright: RCAHMS)

for the leader has curls and a longer beard, a striped or fringed border to his robe, a more decorative shield and a larger spear. The third warrior lacks a beard, perhaps to denote his youth or junior status. We shall never know whether the sculptor was portraying a particular ruler in the leading warlord, but this powerful vignette certainly conveys an impression of an ordered and stable society in Orkney in the 8th century.

That society was Christian, yet there is no overt reference to the Church among the small number of surviving Pictish symbol stones from Orkney. All that remains to recall the early Church are small cross-incised grave-markers (including two inscribed stones), one large cross-slab and a couple of possible fragments, and the front panel of an altar with a decorative cross from the island of Flotta. Were the rest destroyed by an incoming pagan force in the shape of the Norwegian Vikings who took over the islands in the course of the 9th century?

Present location

Museum of Scotland, Chambers Street, Edinburgh. Cast on site.

References

RCAHMS 1946 *Inventory of Orkney*, no 1, 4–5.

Henderson, G & Henderson, I 2004 *The Art of the Picts*, 57, 179. London: Thames & Hudson.

Ritchie, A 1989 *Picts*, 52–4. Edinburgh: HMSO.

Ritchie, J N Graham 2003 'Pictish art in Orkney, *in* Downes, J & Ritchie, A (eds) *Sea Change: Orkney and Northern Europe in the later Iron Age AD 300-800*, 117–26. Balgavies, Angus: The Pinkfoot Press.

Young and old from Jarlshof

People have lived at Jarlshof, beside the sheltered bay, the West Voe of Sumburgh, at the southern end of Shetland on and off since the third millennium BC. The stone foundations of their houses survive, along with a wealth of everyday tools, but the closest link with the people themselves is a small piece of slate carved with the portraits of two men, one young and one old. Both are beautifully drawn, clearly from life, by an assured hand using a finely pointed metal implement.

Sir Walter Scott visited the ruins of the old laird's house at Sumburgh in 1814, and he used it as a setting in his novel, *The Pirate*, with the invented, and predictive, name of Jarlshof. The archaeological site beneath Jarlshof was discovered in 1897 after severe storms had eroded the shore and exposed the remains of stone walls, and it did indeed prove to include Norse remains. John Bruce, whose family had owned the land since 1592, carried out excavations over the next eight years, and in 1925 the site was taken

32 *The older man* (© Trustees of the National Museums of Scotland)

into state care. More excavations took place in the 1930s and 1940s, and it was in the final season of digging under John Hamilton in 1951 that the portrait slate was found amongst domestic rubbish of early Viking times.

The fragment is only 115mm by 76mm, and part of the old man's portrait is missing but the young man's portrait is complete. A handsome man with a well-shaped nose and large eye, he has a neatly trimmed moustache and beard, and his hair is drawn back from his face to form a row of curls in profile from his forehead to the nape of his neck. No attempt has been made to show the ear, though it must have been visible. There are two parallel lines high at the neck, which may represent the collar of his garment but they also protrude in front as if he is a prisoner forced to wear a neck-shackle. A crude sketch of a hen or a duck appears to be the work of a different hand. On the other side of the slate is part of the face, again in profile, of an older man, with a wispy

59

look about his hair and beard, a bulbous nose, sunken eye and just a hint of toothlessness about the mouth. There is also an outline sketch of a basking seal on this side.

Who were these men and who was the artist? If in the younger man we are meant to see a prisoner, he is likely to have been a slave taken on a Viking raid, perhaps a Pict. The older man was perhaps someone who had lived on the farm all his life, whether a native Shetlander or a Norseman. The artist was almost certainly a Pict and one conversant with the art-style of Pictish figure-carving, for graffiti such as this are familiar from native sites in Scotland (especially Inchmarnock, Bute) and Ireland, and the profiled face with large almond-shaped eye can be found on Pictish carved stones. As Robert Stevenson first recognised, the young man with his curls is particularly close in style to the leading warlord on the Brough of Birsay slab.

These portraits are among a series of slate-incised graffiti from similar levels at Jarlshof. They include ships with rigging, oars and steering rudder, a dragon-head, an archer with a cross-bow, animals, interlace and parts of grids that may represent tally slates or gaming boards. Most are little more than doodles, but some, like the portraits, are the sensitive work of a true artist.

Present location

Museum of Scotland, Edinburgh.

References

Hamilton, J R C 1956 *Excavations at Jarlshof, Shetland*, 114–15, 121. Edinburgh: HMSO.
Stevenson, R B K 1981 'Christian sculpture in Norse Shetland', *Froðskaparrit*, 28/29 (1981), 283–92.

Shetland hoods

Two remarkably similar hooded figures have been found in Shetland and are as yet unique to Shetland. One was a casual find from Mail on the east coast of the south mainland and the other came from an excavation at Upper Scalloway in central mainland, and their discoveries were almost three decades apart. Each is carved in the round of stone in the form of a flat-based cone depicting a human figure dressed in a full-length robe with a hood, with only the face visible and the hood drawn close around it. They differ only in the treatment of the face. The Mail figure has the hood tucked in around the face, and the face itself looks almost brutal or mask-like, with slits for the eyes and mouth and a flat squared-off nose. A horizontal line across the upper forehead may represent the hairline. By contrast, the Scalloway face peers out from a hood that covers the jawline entirely, though the eyes and mouth are similarly delineated as slits, and the nose, though equally prominent, has a more human and less helmet-like outline. Here the forehead is a triangle with holes at each angle, and it is clear that a decorative plate is missing. It might have been an amber stud or glass stud or a tiny gilded bronze plaque, but we shall never know.

The Mail figure was found by a local crofter while removing stones from the broch of Mail, and it was presented to the National Museum of Antiquities of Scotland in Edinburgh in 1923 by James M Goudie, a Corresponding Member of the Society of Antiquaries of Scotland and a JP in Lerwick. The broch of Mail lies on a tidal islet at Cunningsburgh, and it was in the nearby graveyard that the Shaman of Mail was found. The little hooded figure is 42mm high and 20mm in diameter at the base, and it differs from its Scalloway brother in that the hood is peaked at the back.

Archaeological excavations on another broch site at Upper Scalloway took place over the winter months of 1989/1990 in gruelling weather conditions. Despite rain, snow and gale-force winds, a picture emerged of an Iron Age broch around which occupation continued into Pictish times, and the hooded figure was found in a level that was radiocarbon-dated to the period AD 500-900. It is fractionally taller than its Mail counterpart, at 43mm high and 20mm in diameter at the base, but they were surely both designed for the same purpose. A minor difference can be seen in that there is a small hole in the base, perhaps

33 *The Mail figure* (© Niall Sharples)

relating to the manufacture of the piece rather than to any former peg. More important is the fact that this figure was painted with a manganese-rich material that now appears dark brown but may originally have been red in colour.

What are these two hooded figures? They are usually interpreted as gaming pieces, and the fact that the Scalloway figure was painted may support that idea, for any board game for two players with similar pieces (as in draughts and chess) needs a different colour for each team. The Scalloway excavations also yielded three other damaged conical pieces and a truncated conical piece with a linear interlace design incised into its top, all of which could be seen as playing pieces. There were also three complete and two fragmentary dice. But dice can be used for games not involving other playing pieces, and no gaming boards were found in the Scalloway excavations.

Is it possible that we are assuming these two hooded figures to be playing pieces because we are familiar with the figures associated with the game of

34 *The Scalloway figure* (© Niall Sharples)

chess? Chess was not played in Europe before the 12th century, but before that there was a similar battle game for two players known from historical sources as *hnefetafl* among the Norsemen and *brandubh* among the native Welsh and Irish. These hooded figures may relate to such games, but is it not also possible that they are nothing to do with board games and everything to do with shamans' equipment?

Present location

The Mail piece is in the Museum of Scotland, Chambers Street, Edinburgh, and the Scalloway piece is in the Shetland Museum, Lerwick.

References

Proc Soc Antiq Scot, 48 (1923-4), 17.

Sharples, Niall 1998 *Scalloway: a broch, Late Iron Age and Medieval Cemetery*. Oxford: Oxbow Monograph 82.

35 *The larger mount from Crieff* (© Trustees of the National Museums of Scotland)

Gentleman of Crieff

Outstanding skill created this superb mount somewhere in Pictland around AD 800. The eye is drawn instantly to the bearded human face with its sleepy gaze and enigmatic smile, and, as Michael Spearman observed, 'in the serious world of Insular art' the Crieff mount is 'a rare example of warmth and happiness.' It was acquired, along with a smaller mount of similar shape but lacking the face, in Crieff by Mrs Hugh W Young of Athole House, Bridge of Allan (whose husband dug at the Pictish fort of Burghead on the Moray coast), and the two mounts were given to the National Mueum of Antiquities in Edinburgh in 1889. They appear to have been part of a hoard, for two years later Mrs Young gave the Museum a plain bronze harness-loop, which belonged to the same group of objects as the mounts, but unfortunately there is no record of exactly where the hoard was found or of whether there were more than three items. The find-spot is likely to have been local to Strathearn, and Crieff is not so very far upstream from the Pictish royal centre at Forteviot. The two mounts certainly belong to a world of wealthy aristocratic patrons.

Measuring 58mm by 55mm, the face-mount illustrated here was cast in good-quality bronze (copper-alloy) and finished with heavy gilding, and domed studs were inserted into three roundels, one of clear glass in the centre and two flanking it of amber or some amber-coloured material. The background to the high-relief decoration is filled with ribbon interlace in low relief. The serene face is protected by two birds, whose legs frame the lower part of the face and whose wings arch back from scroll joints at the shoulder. The amber studs form the eyes of griffins, part-lion as seen from the ear and part-eagle as shown by the beak. Both the griffins and the face between birds are images that reveal potentially Christian connotations. The remains of three fastenings survive on the back of the mount, but there is no clue as to what was attached, though a bronze bowl, a book-cover or a wooden casket are all possible. The curve at the base of the mount implies that it may have been part of a set that was originally arranged around a central roundel.

Whatever its original function, the mount was eventually re-used for another purpose, perhaps on horse harness, by drilling two holes through the background interlace and inserting new bronze rivets. Particularly if it was originally on an item of Church equipment, such re-use is very unlikely in a Christian community, and it may be that the Crieff mounts and the harness-loop were part of a hoard of Viking loot. There were Viking raids into the heart of Pictland in the 860s that may give us the social context for both the re-use of the mounts and their secret disposal in a hoard that lay undetected until the 19th century.

Present location

Museum of Scotland, Chambers Street, Edinburgh.

References

Anon 1890 'Donations to the Museum', *Proc Soc Antiq Scot*, 23 (1889-90), 122–3.

Spearman, R Michael 1993 'The mounts from Crieff, Perthshire, and their wider context', *in* Spearman, R M & Higgitt, J (eds) *The Age of Migrating Ideas: early medieval art in Northern Britain and Scotland*, 135–42. Stroud: Alan Sutton Publishing Ltd/NMS.

36 *Detail of the larger mount from Crieff* (© Trustees of the National Museums of Scotland)

A king remembered at Dupplin

37 *The Dupplin cross on the hillside at Bankhead* (© Tom & Sybil Gray Collection)

Skirting the flood plain of the River Earn, as close as possible to its confluence with the Water of May, lay one of the most important power-centres of early medieval Scotland. This was Forteviot, a royal palace for both Pictish and Scottish kings, where the famed Kenneth mac Alpin died around AD 858. Forteviot was destined to be eclipsed by Scone, though it seems to have remained a royal residence into the 12th century, and today's agrarian landscape gives no hint of its former glory. Aerial photographs show, however, a startling complexity of buried archaeological sites ranging from prehistoric ritual monuments to high-status Pictish burials south and east of the modern village of Forteviot, and the focus of the palace buildings may have been beneath and to the north of the village. That the palace included a sophisticated stone-built church is known from a carved stone arch, dating to the 9th century, which was found in the Water of May sometime before 1832 and can be seen in the

Museum of Scotland in Edinburgh. Equidistant from the palace and on higher ground were two great stone crosses, one to the south-east at Invermay and one to the north at Dupplin. Only fragments remain of the Invermay cross, which was 'wantonly destroyed' some years before Romilly Allen visited its site in 1891, but the Dupplin cross has survived gloriously intact.

Until 1998, the Dupplin cross stood on the hillside above and on the north side of the River Earn at Bankhead. It would scarcely have been visible from Forteviot, but it would have acted as a royal signpost for travellers making their way by boat to the palace. Carved from a single slab of sandstone, it rose 2.62m above its socket stone and another 0.24m at its base was set into the socket, less than one tenth of its total height.

This is a sturdy cross with robust decoration that celebrates kingship and underlines the military power of the king, and its message was plain for all to see and understand. Both faces and both sides of the cross are decorated, including three motifs illustrating the life of the biblical King David (shepherd, bear-slayer and harpist) which provide a model of kingship. The vine-scroll ornament on the cross-head, together with a pattern of Columban doves on the west face, links the earthly king with the Church.

It is very tempting to view the horseborne warrior in pride of place beneath the cross-head on the east face as a portrait of the king, his splendid moustache adding a gravitas that is missing from the tightly ranked young warriors in the panel below. If they are over-tall to convey an elite bodyguard, the head of the king is similarly exaggerated in size to emphasise his social pre-eminence. Who was this fine king? A panel in the same position immediately beneath the cross-head on the west face bears the weathered remains of a seven-line Latin inscription. It was recognised for the first time in 1990 by Katherine Forsyth, when a high-quality cast of the cross was made by the National Museums of Scotland for an exhibition, which allowed the cast to be studied indoors under ideal light conditions. Most of the inscription remains

38 *The east face of the cross*
(drawing by Ian G Scott, Crown Copyright: Historic Scotland)

undeciphered, but the first two lines appear to read 'Custantin filius Fircus', who is identifiable with Constantine son of Fergus, King of the Picts from 789 until his death in 820, and simultaneously King of Dalriada for the last ten years. The cross is thus likely to have been commissioned either by Constantine himself or by his successor. This inscription transforms the Dupplin cross into a unique intact and documented survivor of an early medieval Scottish royal estate.

A postscript is required to explain the recent history of this remarkable cross. The threat from erosion and the need to move the cross indoors had been clear for many years but the ideal new location was far from clear, though the National Museums of Scotland were keen to acquire the cross for the new Museum of Scotland. A public enquiry was held and eventually the cross was taken into care by the Secretary of State for Scotland. In the short term a compromise was reached whereby the cross was to be displayed in the Museum of Scotland for three years from its opening in 1998 and thereafter in St Serf's Church in Dunning in the care of Historic Scotland. Dunning was chosen as the nearest available place to the original location at Dupplin. Posterity will judge whether the right decision was made, for it must be admitted that, in its new home, relatively few people will see this astonishing survival from twelve centuries ago.

39 *The royal horseman* (drawing by Ian G Scott; Crown Copyright: Historic Scotland)

Present location

St Serf's Church, Dunning, Perthshire (Historic Scotland; open only in summer).

References

Forsyth, Katherine 1995 'The inscriptions on the Dupplin Cross', *in* Bourke, C (ed) *From the Isles of the North: early medieval art in Ireland and Britain*, 237–44. Belfast: HMSO.

Henderson, Isabel 1999 'The Dupplin Cross: a preliminary consideration of its art-historical context', *in* Hawkes, J & Mills, S (eds) *Northumbria's Golden Age*, 161–77. Stroud: Alan Sutton Publishing.

40 *The back of the Invergowrie cross-slab* (drawing by Ian G Scott; Crown Copyright: RCAHMS)

The ruined 16th-century church at Invergowrie west of Dundee was dedicated, as were its predecessors, to St Peter, and it is thought that an ecclesiastical presence here may go back to a foundation by St Boniface in the 7th century. The oval shape of the graveyard enclosure suggests an early date, as do its location on a low knoll beside a burn and close to the shore of the Firth of Tay and the discovery in the graveyard of two upright cross-slabs of the 10th century. One appears to have been trimmed for re-use as building material, probably in the 12th-century parish church, but the other has lost only the basal portion that would have been underground and a little of its decoration and this is the stone featured here.

It is a well-designed and carefully executed piece of stone-carving. The sandstone slab is now 0.84m high and probably stood almost a metre high in its original location as a gravestone, and the sculptor dressed it to taper from a width of 0.53m at the top to about 0.4m at the foot. The cross fills the entire panel in a geometric layout with a ring and panels on either side of the upper arm and of the shaft, and all these elements are decorated, as is the outer border. The main interest of the slab lies in the two panels of low-relief carving on the back, which combine very stiff and formal figural and zoomorphic motifs. In the upper panel stand three robed figures facing outwards, with their slippered feet turned to be seen in profile. All three heads are disproportionately large but that of the central figure is more markedly so than those of his companions – the message is clear, these are important people and the one in the middle is really very important. Their tonsured hair, formally draped robes and the books that they carry imply that these are men of the Church, and again the importance of the central figure is emphasised by a larger book and an extra item thought by some to be a seal matrix suspended from a rod. If so, this may be a bishop flanked by two lesser clerics. Others believe the object to be a key and its bearer to be St Peter with the key to the gates of Heaven, and the idea links very neatly with the dedication of the church. The flanking figures have large cross-decorated discs on their shoulders, which may be brooches but are more likely to be embroidered roundels, for brooches are normally shown with their fastening pins (see the Lady of Cadboll).

Beneath these fine characters are two very interesting animals. They have bird's or possibly reptile's feet, elongated bodies with double outlines and curled tufts of hair like manes along their backs, protuberant eyes and long corrugated snouts. Each is rearing up on its hind legs, with a spiral to show the hip, and each has the end of the other's tail between its bared fangs. The style of these animals relates them to Anglo-Scandinavian sculpture of the late 9th and 10th centuries in Yorkshire and suggests that the contacts between communities in eastern Scotland and Yorkshire that facilitated the northern spread of hogback grave-monuments also influenced the decorative art of upright gravestones.

Bishop or saint or both? Another possible identification of the central figure is St Boniface. A 17th-century source claims that 'the venerable bishop' Boniface 'was carried in a boat into the Firth of Tay, to the mouth of the little river, which now separates the district of Gowrie from Angus', where he built a church dedicated to St Peter. This can only be Invergowrie, and it is possible that this late source records a much older tradition linking Bishop Boniface with this early ecclesiastical site. Perhaps some wealthy patron of the 10th century wished not only to show a fashionable taste in sculpture but also to invoke a famous bishop of whom the Invergowrie community was rightly proud.

Present location

Museum of Scotland, Chambers Street, Edinburgh.

References

Henderson, G & Henderson, I 2004 *The Art of the Picts*, 57, 182. London: Thames & Hudson.

MacDonald, Aidan 1992 *Curadán, Boniface and the early church of Rosemarkie*. Rosemarkie: Groam House Museum.